First Published in the UK in 2014 by Focus Education (UK) Ltd

Focus Education (UK) Ltd
Talking Point Conference and Exhibition Centre
Huddersfield Road
Scouthead
Saddleworth
OL4 4AG

Focus Education (UK) Ltd Reg. No 4507968

ISBN 978-1-909038-36-3

Companies, institutions and other organisations wishing to make bulk purchases of books published by
Focus Education should contact their local bookstore or Focus Education direct:

Customer Services, Focus Education, Talking Point Conference and Exhibition Centre,
Huddersfield Road, Scouthead, Saddleworth, OL4 4AG
Tel 01457 821818 Fax 01457 878205

www.focus-education.co.uk
customerservice@focus-education.co.uk
Printed in Great Britain by Focus Education UK Ltd, Scouthead

Users should be fully aware that Ofsted may change any element of their descriptors and guidance.
This document was wholly accurate at the date of publication.

About the author

Simon Camby is the Chief Executive of the Focus Academy Trust. Prior to this, Simon was a Director at Focus Education.

Simon has a well-established track record in education which includes work as a headteacher, senior local authority adviser and lead Ofsted inspector. The inspection in his most recent headship acknowledged:

- *'The headteacher has the respect of the local community and, as a result, parents are overwhelmingly supportive of the school.'*
- *'The determination of the headteacher and leadership team to enhance the pupils' quality of education is in evidence throughout the school and provides the inspiration from which all staff gain strength.'*
- *His strong and inspirational leadership provides clear educational direction, as a result rapid progress has been made in addressing the many weaknesses identified at the time of the last inspection.'*

Simon has written a wide range of publications which adopt a clear and user-friendly style.

Simon is well established as a consultant and his work is highly valued by school and LA leaders both in England and overseas. His main areas of work link to quality leadership, improving learning, quality assessment and curriculum innovation. He works with colleagues in school to help drive their improvements as well as leading conferences and training across England and with international schools. Simon also has a small number of clients who he works with as a leadership coach. He is an accredited Myers Briggs (MBTI) practitioner and uses this as a tool in leadership coaching and leadership team development work. Simon has undertaken Ofsted inspection training and inspects under the current framework.

Recent feedback from delegates who attended training led by Simon notes:

- *'The best training I have ever attended.'* (Primary head)
- *'Everyone commented on the quality of the training. Everyone felt confident to contribute. We are totally fired up! Thank you.'* (Infant head)
- *'Simon broke everything down so that it made perfect sense. I have so many practical tools that can be used straight away.'* (Teacher)
- *'Wow! Once again a fantastic, provoking and brilliant day. The staff feel reinvigorated. Thank you.'* (Headteacher)
- *'Highly professional in approach. Managed the needs of the diverse audience superbly.'* (LA Head of School Improvement)

Leading geography in your school

Contents

Being the subject leader

This section outlines some of the key elements of being the subject leader in your school.

Subject leader role

Subject leaders provide professional leadership for a subject or group of subjects.

Key purpose
Accelerate progress and raise standards through securing high quality teaching, a rich curriculum and effective use of resources.

Elements of the role
- Knowing how well children make progress and what the standards are.
- Ensuring that teaching within the subject is strong and promotes good learning.
- Evaluating all aspects of the subject and summarising to define next steps for improvement.
- Action planning for future development and evaluating whether actions have a demonstrable impact.
- Ensuring that appropriate resources are in place to deliver a rich and challenging curriculum.
- Having oversight of curriculum coverage and ensuring the curriculum meets national requirements.
- Providing guidance and support to colleagues.
- Leading professional development
- Overseeing the effectiveness of assessment.
- Promoting the subject and taking a proactive and inspirational stance with staff and pupils.
- Monitoring the effectiveness of teaching and the impact on learning and progress.
- Making best use of financial and human resources to impact on progress.

Getting the role in perspective

There are many people who still do not understand the central strand of subject leadership. All too often, the role is confined to tidying cupboards and labelling resources! Whilst this is important and has a place, it is important that subject leaders grasp the core purpose of the role and focus on answering a few key questions:

➢ How high are standards?
➢ How well are children progressing?
➢ Is this good enough?
➢ How effective is teaching, including assessment?
➢ Is it good enough?
➢ How well planned is the curriculum to raise standards and promote fundamental British values?
➢ Is it good enough?
➢ How effective is leadership and management?
➢ Is it good enough?

Underpinning each of these would be the sub-questions...

✧ How do you know?
✧ What next?

The diagram on the next page summarises the mind-set for subject leaders to focus these key questions.

Whatever your subject…

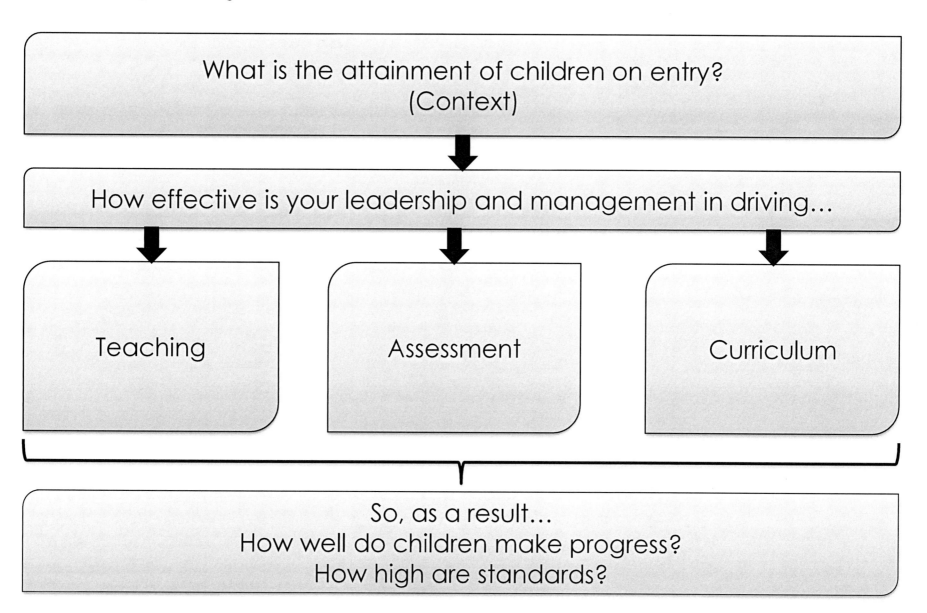

What is the attainment of children on entry?
(Context)

How effective is your leadership and management in driving…

Teaching

Assessment

Curriculum

So, as a result…
How well do children make progress?
How high are standards?

Statutory
Curriculum Coverage

This section outlines the geography curriculum as outlined in the National Curriculum 2014.

What the National Curriculum requires in geography at KS1

Locational knowledge
- Name and locate the world's seven continents and five oceans
- Name, locate and identify characteristics of the four countries and capital cities of the United Kingdom and its surrounding seas

⟧ Locational knowledge

Place knowledge
- Understand geographical similarities and differences through studying the human and physical geography of a small area of the United Kingdom, and of a small area in a contrasting non-European country

⟧ Place knowledge

Human and physical geography
- Identify seasonal and daily weather patterns in the United Kingdom and the location of hot and cold areas of the world in relation to the Equator and the North and South Poles
- Use basic geographical vocabulary to refer to:
  - Key physical features, including: beach, cliff, coast, forest, hill, mountain, sea, ocean, river, soil, valley, vegetation, season and weather
  - Key human features, including: city, town, village, factory, farm, house, office, port, harbour and shop

⟧ Human & physical geography

Geographical skills and fieldwork
- Use world maps, atlases and globes to identify the United Kingdom and its countries, as well as the countries, continents and oceans studied at this key stage
- Use simple compass directions (North, South, East and West) and locational and directional language [for example, near and far; left and right], to describe the location of features and routes on a map
- Use aerial photographs and plan perspectives to recognise landmarks and basic human and physical features; devise a simple map; and use and construct basic symbols in a key
- Use simple fieldwork and observational skills to study the geography of their school and its grounds and the key human and physical features of its surrounding environment.

⟧ Geographical skills & fieldwork

What the National Curriculum requires in geography at KS2

Department for Education

Locational knowledge
- Locate the world's countries, using maps to focus on Europe (including the location of Russia) and North and South America, concentrating on their environmental regions, key physical and human characteristics, countries, and major cities
- Name and locate counties and cities of the United Kingdom, geographical regions and their identifying human and physical characteristics, key topographical features (including hills, mountains, coasts and rivers), and land-use patterns; and understand how some of these aspects have changed over time
- Identify the position and significance of latitude, longitude, Equator, Northern Hemisphere, Southern Hemisphere, the Tropics of Cancer and Capricorn, Arctic and Antarctic Circle, the Prime/Greenwich Meridian and time zones (including day and night)

Locational knowledge

Place knowledge
- Understand geographical similarities and differences through the study of human and physical geography of a region of the United Kingdom, a region in a European country, and a region within North or South America

Place knowledge

Human and physical geography
- Describe and understand key aspects of:
    o Physical geography, including: climate zones, biomes and vegetation belts, rivers, mountains, volcanoes and earthquakes, and the water cycle
    o Human geography, including: types of settlement and land use, economic activity including trade links, and the distribution of natural resources including energy, food, minerals and water

Human & physical geography

Geographical skills and fieldwork
- Use maps, atlases, globes and digital/computer mapping to locate countries and describe features studied
- Use the eight points of a compass, four and six-figure grid references, symbols and key (including the use of Ordnance Survey maps) to build their knowledge of the United Kingdom and the wider world
- Use fieldwork to observe, measure, record and present the human and physical features in the local area using a range of methods, including sketch maps, plans and graphs, and digital technologies.

Geographical skills & fieldwork

Quick Check:
The geography curriculum

This section enables school leaders to evaluate their curriculum to ensure there will be full coverage of the statutory requirements (based on National Curriculum 2014).

Subject content from the programme of study	What are our geographical themes or unit titles? (Content may be split between themes or units)	When will pupils be taught this?	Links with other subjects?	Opportunities for pupils to apply basic skills
Pupils should be taught to name and locate the world's seven continents and five oceans.				
Pupils should be taught to name, locate and identify characteristics of the four countries and capital cities of the United Kingdom and its surrounding seas.				
Pupils should be taught to understand geographical similarities and differences through studying the human and physical geography of a small area of the United Kingdom, and of a small area in a contrasting non-European country.				
Pupils should be taught to identify seasonal and daily weather patterns in the United Kingdom and the location of hot and cold areas of the world in relation to the Equator and the North and South Poles.				
Pupils should be taught to use basic geographical vocabulary to refer to key physical features, including: beach, cliff, coast, forest, hill, mountain, sea, ocean, river, soil, valley, vegetation, season and weather.				

Subject content from the programme of study	What are our geographical themes or unit titles? (Content may be split between themes or units)	When will pupils be taught this?	Links with other subjects?	Opportunities for pupils to apply basic skills
Pupils should be taught to use basic geographical vocabulary to refer to key human features, including: city, town, village, factory, farm, house, office, port, harbour and shop.				
Pupils should be taught to use world maps, atlases and globes to identify the United Kingdom and its countries, as well as the countries, continents and oceans studied at this key stage.				
Pupils should be taught to use simple compass directions (North, South, East and West) and locational and directional language [for example, near and far; left and right], to describe the location of features and routes on a map.				

Curriculum enrichments (visits, visitors, themed events etc.)

Subject content from the programme of study	What are our geographical themes or unit titles? (Content may be split between themes or units)	When will pupils be taught this?	Links with other subjects?	Opportunities for pupils to apply basic skills
Pupils should be taught to locate the world's countries, using maps to focus on Europe (including the location of Russia) and North and South America, concentrating on their environmental regions, key physical and human characteristics, countries, and major cities.				
Pupils should be taught to name and locate counties and cities of the United Kingdom, geographical regions and their identifying human and physical characteristics, key topographical features (including hills, mountains, coasts and rivers), and land-use patterns; and understand how some of these aspects have changed over time.				
Pupils should be taught to identify the position and significance of latitude, longitude, Equator, Northern Hemisphere, Southern Hemisphere, the Tropics of Cancer and Capricorn, Arctic and Antarctic Circle, the Prime/Greenwich Meridian and time zones (including day and night)				
Pupils should be taught to understand geographical similarities and differences through the study of human and physical geography of a region of the United Kingdom, a region in a European country, and a region within North or South America.				
Pupils should be taught to describe and understand key aspects of physical geography, including: climate zones, biomes and vegetation belts, rivers, mountains, volcanoes and earthquakes, and the water cycle.				

Subject content from the programme of study	What are our geographical themes or unit titles? (Content may be split between themes or units)	When will pupils be taught this?	Links with other subjects?	Opportunities for pupils to apply basic skills
Pupils should be taught to describe and understand key aspects of human geography, including: types of settlement and land use, economic activity including trade links, and the distribution of natural resources including energy, food, minerals and water.				
Pupils should be taught to use maps, atlases, globes and digital/computer mapping to locate countries and describe features studied.				
Pupils should be taught to use the eight points of a compass, four and six-figure grid references, symbols and key (including the use of Ordnance Survey maps) to build their knowledge of the United Kingdom and the wider world.				
Pupils should be taught to use fieldwork to observe, measure, record and present the human and physical features in the local area using a range of methods, including sketch maps, plans and graphs, and digital technologies.				

Curriculum enrichments (visits, visitors, themed events etc.)

Key Assessment Criteria

The key assessment criteria for geography have been devised in such a way that they can be applied in all settings, regardless of the agreed programme of study. These criteria allow teachers to assess how well children are developing as geographers. Teachers may wish to supplement these key assessment criteria with other criteria if they feel that this adds value.

In devising the key assessment criteria, judgements had to be made about what is considered age appropriate in line with the key stage programmes of study. These have been tested and evaluated by class teachers. In presenting these criteria, there is no suggestion that this is the only 'correct' sequence; but rather a suggestion to help teachers plan and assess.

Key Assessment Criteria: *Being a geographer*

A year 1 geographer	A year 2 geographer	A year 3 geographer
• I can keep a weather chart and answer questions about the weather.	• I can say what I like and do not like about the place I live in.	• I can use the correct geographical words to describe a place.
• I can explain where I live and tell someone my address.	• I can say what I like and do not like about a different place.	• I can use some basic Ordnance Survey map symbols.
• I can explain some of the main things that are in hot and cold places.	• I can describe a place outside Europe using geographical words.	• I can use grid references on a map.
• I can explain the clothes that I would wear in hot and cold places.	• I can describe some of the features of an island.	• I can use an atlas by using the index to find places.
• I can explain how the weather changes throughout the year and name the seasons.	• I can describe the key features of a place from a picture using words like beach, coast, forest, hill, mountain, ocean, valley.	• I can describe how volcanoes are created.
• I can name the four countries in the United Kingdom and locate them on a map.	• I can explain how jobs may be different in other locations.	• I can locate and name some of the world's most famous volcanoes.
• I can name some of the main towns and cities in the United Kingdom.	• I can explain how an area has been spoilt or improved and give my reasons.	• I can describe how earthquakes are created.
	• I can explain the facilities that a village, town and city may need and give reasons.	• I can name a number of countries in the northern hemisphere.
	• I can name the continents of the world and locate them on a map.	• I can name and locate the capital cities of neighbouring European countries.
	• I can name the world oceans and locate them on a map.	
	• I can name the capital cities of England, Wales, Scotland and Ireland.	
	• I can find where I live on a map of the United Kingdom.	

Key Assessment Criteria: *Being a geographer*

A year 4 geographer	A year 5 geographer	A year 6 geographer
• I can carry out research to discover features of villages, towns or cities. • I can plan a journey to a place in England. • I can collect and accurately measure information (e.g. rainfall, temperature, wind speed, noise levels etc.). • I can explain why people may be attracted to live in cities. • I can explain why people may choose to live in one place rather than another. • I can locate the Tropic of Cancer and Tropic of Capricorn. • I can explain the difference between the British Isles, Great Britain and the United Kingdom. • I know the countries that make up the European Union. • I can find at least six cities in the UK on a map. • I can name and locate some of the main islands that surround the United Kingdom. • I can name the areas of origin of the main ethnic groups in the United Kingdom and in our school.	• I can plan a journey to a place in another part of the world, taking account of distance and time. • I can explain why many cities are situated on or close to rivers. • I can explain why people are attracted to live by rivers. • I can explain the course of a river. • I can name and locate many of the world's most famous rivers in an atlas. • I can name and locate many of the world's most famous mountainous regions in an atlas. • I can explain how a location fits into its wider geographical location with reference to human and economical features.	• I can use Ordnance Survey symbols and 6 figure grid references. • I can answer questions by using a map. • I can use maps, aerial photographs, plans and e-resources to describe what a locality might be like. • I can describe how some places are similar and dissimilar in relation to their human and physical features. • I can name the largest desert in the world and locate desert regions in an atlas. • I can identify and name the Tropics of Cancer and Capricorn as well as the Arctic and Antarctic Circles. • I can explain how time zones work and calculate time differences around the world.

Assessment Template

This section provides a simple template that school leaders can use to record the outcomes of their assessment.

Assessment and tracking

<u>Basic level</u>

It is important that you have secure knowledge of how well pupils are attaining in relation to expectations. As the National Curriculum only defines end of key stage expectations for geography, you need to be clear about your milestones for each year group. A possible suggestion for this is included earlier in this publication.

Essentially, you need to know whether pupils are:

- Below the expectation
- Meeting the expectation
- Exceeding the expectation

The chart on the next page would help you record this. It is suggested that you have one chart like this for each cohort in your school (i.e. it follows the cohort as they progress). This means that you can compare their year-on-year progress; noting you will need to take account of changes to the cohort.

<u>Digging deeper</u>

In order to take your tracking and evaluation to a deeper level, it would be helpful to consider pupils groups within your school, e.g. gender, ethnicity, pupil premium, vulnerable groups etc. You need to be exploring whether there are differences in the achievement of different groups.

Cohort tracker for geography

	Year 1	Year 2	Year 3	Year 4	Year 5	Year 6
Below expectations						
Meeting expectations						
Exceeding expectations						

Achievement in geography

	Strengths	Next steps
Standards by the end of KS1		
Standards by the end of KS2		
Achievement judgement		
Use of English skills in geography		
Use of mathematics skills in geography		
Use of computing skills in geography		

Achievement in geography

	Strengths	Next steps
How well are gaps being narrowed between vulnerable groups?		
Other issues		

Evaluating geography

This section enables school leaders to evaluate their geography curriculum and arrive at an overall judgment for the quality of their setting's curriculum.

Evaluating geography in your school

There are criteria for the areas identified in the diagram below.

It is important that the criteria are not used a checklist.
They must be applied adopting a 'best fit' approach.

Note that if any element is inadequate, it is likely that the overall judgement will be inadequate.

Leaders may find it helpful to highlight text.

This evaluation can then be used to
Identify next steps for improvement.

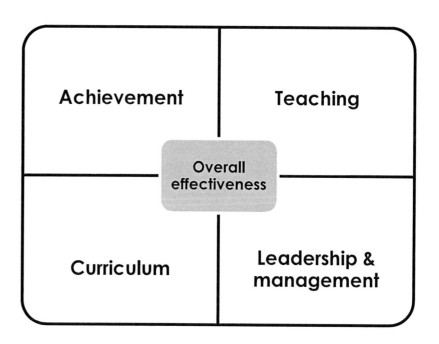

Achievement of pupils in geography

Outstanding	• Pupils have excellent knowledge of where places are and what they are like. They have excellent understanding of the ways in which places are interdependent and interconnected and how human and physical environments are interrelated. • Pupils have an extensive base of core geographical knowledge and vocabulary. • Pupils are able to carry out increasingly complex geographical enquiry, apply questioning skills and use effective analytical and presentational techniques in a wide range of environments, scales and contexts. They reach clear conclusions and are able to develop reasoned arguments to explain their findings. • Pupils are able to think for themselves and take the initiative in, for example, asking questions, carrying out their own investigations and working constructively with others. They show significant levels of originality, imagination or creativity in their understanding and skills within the subject. • Fieldwork and other geographical skills, including numerical and quantitative skills, and techniques are highly developed and frequently utilised. • Pupils develop passion and commitment to the subject and exhibit a real sense of curiosity in finding out about the world around them and the people who live there. • Pupils are able to express well-balanced opinions, rooted in very good knowledge and understanding about current and contemporary issues in society and the environment.
Good	• Most pupils have a good knowledge of where places are and what they are like. They have a good understanding of the ways in which places are interdependent and interconnected and how human and physical environments are interrelated. • Pupils have a good basis of core geographical knowledge and vocabulary. • Pupils are able to use data and information sources to search and select, organise and investigate, and refine and present information well. • Pupils explore hypotheses which enable them to show good geographical understanding. They are able to reach conclusions and develop generally well-reasoned arguments to explain their findings. • Pupils take the initiative in their work and when working with others. They demonstrate some originality, imagination or creativity in their subject work. • Most pupils acquire and use a range of fieldwork and other geographical skills, including numerical and quantitative skills, and techniques. • The majority of pupils enjoy the subject and can explain its value. Most are interested in the world around them and in contemporary issues in society and the environment, and realise that geography helps us to understand them.
Requires Improvement	• Some pupils may have a good knowledge of where places are and what they are like, others are less clear. They have some understanding of the ways in which places are interdependent and interconnected and how physical and human environments are interrelated. • Pupils have reasonable core geographical knowledge. They make use of some geography-specific terminology, although their subject-specific vocabulary is limited. • Pupils are able to use data and information sources to search and select, investigate and present some findings, often in a simple format. • Pupils occasionally take the initiative in developing their work. Occasionally, pupils show creative or original responses in their subject work. • Most pupils acquire and use some basic fieldwork and other geographical skills, such as numerical and quantitative skills, appropriate to their age, but only at a basic level. • Pupils are able to reach short conclusions and are able to provide some reasons to explain their judgements. They are generally interested in the subject and the world around them.
Inadequate	Achievement is likely to be inadequate if **any** of the following apply. • Pupils' knowledge of places is weak and confused. They have a very weak understanding of the ways in which places are interdependent and interconnected and how physical and human environments are interrelated. • Pupils have weak core geographical knowledge and vocabulary. • The range of geographical skills and techniques to support their presentations is inadequate and often used inappropriately. • Too many pupils fail to work effectively. They give up easily and often fail to complete work. • Most pupils do not make adequate progress in their acquisition and application of fieldwork and other geographical skills. • Pupils do not enjoy geography or find it challenging or stimulating.

Achievement of pupils in geography (self-evaluation)

Best fit judgment	
Evidence for this judgment	
Next steps	

Outstanding	• Teachers communicate enthusiasm and passion about geography to pupils. • They use specialist geographical vocabulary/ terminology confidently and use their excellent knowledge to ensure that pupils have very good understanding of key geographical concepts. • The outside environment – including through fieldwork – is used extremely well to secure high-quality learning. Lessons are carefully structured. A range of innovative resources –especially those linked to topical issues – are used regularly and very effectively to explore a wide range of geographical topics at a range of scales and across a variety of places. • Pupils are engaged and places are brought to life with the aid of multimedia resources. Work in lessons builds on previous learning to ensure progression in geography. • Pupils' interest and a sense of wonder are stimulated through tasks which also help them to make sense of a complex and dynamically changing world. • Very effective use is made of geographical enquiry to encourage questioning, investigation and critical thinking about issues affecting the world and peoples' lives, now and in the future. • Pupils' understanding of diverse places and landscapes is routinely strengthened. • Maps, at a variety of scales, are used frequently as a matter of routine and are an intrinsic part of learning in geography. This ensures that pupils have good spatial awareness and are very secure in their ability to locate the places they are studying. • Very effective use is made of ICT and Geographical Information Systems (where relevant) to promote learning and enable pupils to use data and information sources to search and select, organise and investigate, and refine and present information skilfully. • Teachers have high expectations and a high level of confidence and expertise, in terms of both their specialist and up-to-date knowledge and their understanding of effective learning in the subject. • Teaching ensures that pupils are able to make use of their prior learning in moving their geographical understanding forward; as a result lessons are stimulating and often innovative, with geographical rigour at their core.
Good	• Teachers have a clear understanding of the value of geography and communicate this to pupils effectively. • They plan and teach effective lessons, making use of specialist expertise. An appropriate range of teaching strategies promote good learning across all aspects of the subject. Teaching is informed by knowledge of current good practice in geography • Good use is made of the outside environment and fieldwork to support learning. • A range of topical multi-media resources is available to support learning to develop a good understanding of a range of places and geographical issues. • Tasks set interest pupils in the study of places and help them to make sense of some of the complexities of a dynamically changing world in which they live. • Lessons build up geographical knowledge, skills and understanding over time. • Good use is made of geographical enquiry to support questioning, investigation and thinking about issues affecting the world and people's lives. • Frequent use is made of maps to a variety of scales to support learning well. This ensures that pupils are secure in their ability to locate the places they are studying. • Good use is made of ICT and Geographical Information Systems (where relevant) to promote learning and enable pupils to use data and information sources to search and select, organise and investigate, and refine and present information well.
Requires Improvement	• Teachers understand how to maintain most pupils' interest in geography. • Teachers show some geographical expertise. Pupils show a basic understanding of the geographical concept or issue they are studying because teachers' questioning may elicit basic answers rather than promote more in-depth discussion and explanation. • Lessons do not build sufficiently on previous learning. Tasks set – including through fieldwork – are sometimes mundane and lack challenge. • Resources, including maps, are used and pupils have some idea of where the places they are studying are located. Multi-media resources are available to support learning but are not always used to their full potential. Insufficient use is made of topical issues to strengthen pupils' understanding of 21st-century geography. Only a narrow range of places are studied. • Teaching promotes pupils' skills in geographical enquiry through questioning and investigative activities. Some use is made of ICT and Geographical Information Systems (where relevant) to promote learning, but opportunities for pupils to use data and information sources to search and select, organise and investigate, and refine and present information are limited. • There may be excessive and inappropriate emphasis on a narrow range of examination questions or test skills in secondary schools and an overemphasis on skills in primary schools at the expense of real geographical learning.
Inadequate	Teaching is likely to be inadequate where **any** of the following apply. • Teaching fails to challenge or interest pupils in geography. Teaching over time does not build up pupils' geographical knowledge sufficiently. As a result, pupils' geographical knowledge of the topic is weak. Pupils may be unclear about why they are doing a particular task. • Pupils' use of geographical language and terminology is limited or insecure and their learning may be fragmented or confused because teachers fail to use resources or teaching strategies which secure effective geographical learning. • Pupils' skills in geographical enquiry are insufficiently developed. Pupils have little opportunity to discuss, ask their own questions, challenge ideas or think for themselves. • Little use is made of fieldwork to support learning. There is considerable variation in the frequency and quality of fieldwork experiences between classes. • The context of lessons may be geographical but the focus may not be sufficiently rooted in geographical learning, with the result that subject-specific gains are minimal. • Insufficient or inappropriate use is made of maps. Little use is made of data and pupils are insecure in collecting and analysing them. Presentation skills are poor. • Low-level tasks are set which are inappropriate to the pupils' ages and/or abilities. As a result, the work in their books shows limited progression over time. • Activities occupy pupils rather than extend their learning; opportunities for extended, analytical writing are minimal. • Little use is made of Geographical Information Systems (where relevant).

Quality of teaching in geography (self-evaluation)

Best fit judgment	
Evidence for this judgment	
Next steps	

Outstanding	• The imaginative and stimulating geography curriculum is skilfully designed to match the full range of pupils' needs and to ensure highly effective continuity and progression in their learning. • The key geographical concepts such as place, space, scale, diversity, interdependence and sustainability are clearly embedded in the planning. • The curriculum provides consistently high-quality opportunities for pupils to develop and consolidate the key geographical skills of enquiry, graphicacy and geographical communication. • Fieldwork is well planned and clearly identified as an integral part of the schemes of work. Pupils experience fieldwork on a regular basis, with activities that offer clear progression rather than repetition and include diverse landscapes and varied locations. • The contribution of geography to learning and understanding about current and relevant local, national and global issues is at least good in all major respects, and is exemplary in significant elements. • Excellent links are forged with other agencies and the wider, as well as the global, community to provide a wide range of enrichment activities to promote pupils' learning and engagement with the subject. • Links with other subjects in the school are highly productive in strengthening pupils' learning in geography. • Rigorous curriculum planning ensures that the subject makes an outstanding contribution to pupils' social, moral, spiritual and cultural development.
Good	• The geography curriculum is broad, balanced and well informed by current initiatives in the subject. It is designed to match a range of pupils' needs and ensure effective continuity and progression in their geographical learning. • The key geographical concepts such as place, space, scale, diversity, interdependence and sustainability are clearly identified in the planning. The curriculum provides frequent opportunities for pupils to develop and consolidate key geographical skills of enquiry, graphicacy and geographical communication. • Opportunities for fieldwork are clearly identified and all classes participate in the experience in a variety of locations; it is well used in building up pupils' understanding of related geographical concepts and is linked well into the teaching programme. • Awareness of current and relevant local, national and global issues is planned into the geography curriculum. • Good links are forged with other agencies and the wider and global community to provide a range of enrichment activities to promote pupils' learning and their engagement with the subject. • Links with other subjects in the school strengthen pupils' achievement in geography. • Opportunities to promote pupils' social, moral, spiritual and cultural development are planned and delivered systematically. • The curriculum is broad and balanced, preparing pupils for the opportunities, responsibilities and experiences of later life in modern Britain. • The school can identify how the curriculum promotes fundamental British values of democracy, the rule of law, individual liberty and mutual respect and tolerance of those with different faiths and beliefs.
Requires Improvement	• The geography curriculum secures the pupils' broad and balanced entitlement in the subject and meets any statutory requirements which apply. It provides for a range of pupils' needs and ensures that they make satisfactory progress in their learning. • The key geographical concepts such as place, space, scale, diversity, interdependence and sustainability are identifiable within the planning. • The curriculum provides some limited opportunities for pupils to develop and consolidate aspects of key geographical skills of enquiry, graphicacy and geographical communication. • Some opportunities for fieldwork are identified in the planning, although these may not always be adhered to and there may be variation in fieldwork experiences between classes. Fieldwork in examination classes may be formulaic and focused on meeting examination criteria. Learning about current and relevant local, national and global issues is a part of the geography curriculum, but may not be planned for in such a way as to progressively build up pupils' understanding of the key concepts. • Some links are forged with other agencies and the wider community, although the range of activity provided to enrich pupils' interest and learning may be quite limited. • Links with other subjects contribute to pupils' achievement in geography. • The curriculum ensures that the subject contributes to pupils' social, moral, spiritual and cultural development.
Inadequate	The curriculum in geography is likely to be inadequate if **any** of the following apply. • The geography curriculum does not ensure pupils' entitlement to the subject, may not meet statutory requirements and does not secure continuity in their learning. • It is unclear how the key geographical concepts such as place, space, scale, diversity, interdependence and sustainability are to be progressively developed. • The curriculum provides insufficient and inconsistent opportunities for pupils to develop and consolidate aspects of the key geographical skills of enquiry, graphicacy and geographical communication. • There is little reference in the planning to fieldwork opportunities, with cohorts of pupils getting no or very limited fieldwork experience over a key stage. Fieldwork is not perceived as being important except for meeting examination requirements. • Learning about current and relevant local, national and global issues is fragmented and is not easily identified in the planning. • Opportunities to promote pupils' social, moral, spiritual and cultural development in geography are missed. • There are no links between geography and other subjects in the school. • Enrichment activities have minimal impact in promoting enjoyment and achievement in geography.

Quality of the curriculum in geography (self-evaluation)

Best fit judgment	
Evidence for this judgment	
Next steps	

Quality of leadership in, and management of, geography

Outstanding	• Leadership in geography is informed by a high level of subject expertise and vision. • There is a strong track record of innovation and success. • Out of classroom learning is seen as an entitlement within the subject and is highly promoted by the subject leaders. • Subject reviews, self-evaluation and improvement planning are well informed by current best practice in the subject and in education generally. • Subject leadership inspires confidence and whole-hearted commitment from pupils and colleagues. • There is a shared vision and effective strategies to share good practice and update teachers' subject knowledge through high-quality professional development in the subject. • Geography has a very high profile in the life of the school and is at the cutting edge of initiatives within the school. • The subject makes an excellent contribution to whole-school priorities, including consistent application of literacy and numeracy policies.
Good	• Leadership is well informed by current developments in geography. • Subject reviews, self-evaluation and improvement planning are clearly focused on raising attainment and improving the provision for the subject. • There is a shared common purpose among those involved in teaching the subject, with good opportunities to share practice and access subject training. • Out of classroom learning is seen as an essential component of the subject. • The subject makes a good contribution to whole- school priorities, including literacy and numeracy policies.
Requires Improvement	• Leadership is aware of some current developments in geography, but incorporation of these within its practice may lack sufficient focus. • Provision for the subject is monitored and reviewed regularly. However, this is limited in terms of rigour and robustness. The strengths and priorities for improvement lack sufficient clarity to accelerate improvement. • Out-of-classroom learning may be evident but there is a lack of consistency across the school. • There is some sharing of good practice in geography. However, this is not consistent and is often dependent on the enthusiasm of individual teachers. • There is modest access to subject-specific professional development, although all teachers do not necessarily participate. • The subject contributes to whole-school priorities, including literacy and numeracy policies.
Inadequate	• Geography leadership is not well informed about current initiatives in the subject. It lacks the authority and drive to make a difference. • Key statutory requirements for the subject, such as fieldwork, are not met. • Self-evaluation is weak and not informed by good practice in the subject. • Opportunities for professional development in the subject are limited and, as a result, some staff lack the confidence and expertise to deliver geography effectively. • Geography has a low profile in the life of the school. • The subject makes a minimal contribution to whole-school priorities, including literacy and numeracy policies.

Quality of leadership in, and management of, geography (self-evaluation)

Best fit judgment	
Evidence for this judgment	
Next steps	

The overall effectiveness of geography education provided in the school

Outstanding	• Geography teaching is outstanding and, together with a rich and relevant geography curriculum, contributes to outstanding learning and achievement. Exceptionally, achievement in geography may be good and rapidly improving. • Pupils, and particular groups of pupils, have excellent educational experiences in geography and these ensure that they are very well equipped for the next stage of their education, training or employment. • Pupils' high levels of literacy, appropriate to their age, contribute to their outstanding learning and achievement in geography. • Practice in the subject consistently reflects the highest expectations of staff and the highest aspirations for pupils, including disabled pupils and those with special educational needs. • Best practice is spread effectively in a drive for continuous improvement. • The subject makes an outstanding contribution to pupils' spiritual, moral, social and cultural development.
Good	• Pupils benefit from geography teaching that is at least good and some that is outstanding. This promotes very positive attitudes to learning and ensures that pupils' achievement in geography is at least good. • Pupils and particular groups of pupils have highly positive educational experiences in geography that ensure that they are well prepared for the next stage in their education, training or employment. • Pupils' progress is not held back by an inability to read accurately and fluently. • The school takes effective action to enable most pupils, including disabled pupils and those with special educational needs, to reach their potential in geography. • The subject makes a good contribution to pupils' spiritual, moral, social and cultural development.
Requires Improvement	• Geography in the school requires improvement because one or more of the key judgements for achievement; behaviour and safety (in geography); the quality of teaching; the curriculum; and the quality of leadership and management of geography requires improvement (grade 3).
Inadequate	Geography in the school is likely to be inadequate if inspectors judge any of the following to be inadequate: • the achievement of pupils in geography • the behaviour and safety of pupils in geography • the quality of teaching in geography • the quality of the curriculum in geography • the quality of the leadership in, and management of, geography

The overall effectiveness of geography education provided in the school (self-evaluation)

Best fit judgment	
Evidence for this judgment	
Next steps	

Monitoring
and evaluation

Monitoring and evaluation

Subject leader monitoring is crucial if you are to make judgments about the quality and success of a subject. It is one of the most difficult things to arrange given the time constraints and fact that there are many subjects to monitor.

Senior leaders will need to make decisions about how and when to monitor subjects. This may involve a rolling programme or build on a system of focused and surface monitoring. Your Monitoring and Evaluation Policy will outline clearly which subjects are to be monitored when and by whom.

Monitoring need not be time consuming provided time is well planned and those undertaking the monitoring are prepared to make judgments without too much deliberation.

Critically, before starting, make sure you know:

Are you clear about the difference between monitoring and evaluating?

Whilst this sounds obvious, many people slip into the trap of monitoring without due regard for evaluation. This often means that the monitoring is a complete waste of time as it does not impact on any changes being made.

Monitoring

- Gathering evidence
- Checking

Evaluating

- Asking, 'So what...?'
- What does this mean for next steps?
- What's working well? What needs improving?

You need some kind of monitoring and evaluation in order to assess the **IMPACT** of your actions.

Types of monitoring

There are many ways you can monitor. There is no one right or wrong way. It is important for subject leaders to use their time wisely in order to get the best overview possible. This often means that lesson observations are not a productive way of monitoring due to the time taken.

It is important not to under estimate the usefulness of other types of monitoring which can give you an instant whole school or key stage snap shot. These are some of the ways that subject leaders can find out about what is going on:

Lesson observations	Work sampling/scrutiny
Moderation	Scrutiny of planning
Scrutiny of assessments	Analysing data
Pupil discussion	Discussion with staff
Discussion with parents/carers	Displays
Questionnaires	Pupil shadowing

Monitoring overload

It is obviously important that any monitoring is planned and known about by all staff. This planning is critical in order to ensure that staff do not feel over-burdened with monitoring. If well planned, there is no reason for anyone to feel anxious about subject leader monitoring as it should be helpful in securing a better deal for the children. Some schools have found it useful to use an evidence trail or focused evaluation approach to focus their monitoring and evaluation. This is tried and tested as an effective way of working with subject leaders. When well used it will:

➢ provide clarity of focus;
➢ structure what needs to be done; and
➢ provide a clear framework for recording findings and actions.

The following pages outline a simple overview of this approach.

It is important that agreed actions identify people and timescales in order to hold others to account; i.e. ensuring that all actions are not the sole responsibility of the subject leader.

Steps in using a focused evaluation

1
- Decide the **focus** of the evidence trail.
- Express this as a question.

2
- Be clear **who** is working on the evidence trail and the **time** you have available. This time should include time for monitoring and evaluation.

3
- Decide what **evidence** you are going to gather, i.e. what are you looking at. Be specific: e.g. if you are looking at samples of work, what are you focusing on?

4
- **Do it**.
- Gather the evidence.

MONITORING

5
- **Be evaluative**.
- Ask, 'So what…?'

EVALUATION

6
- Decide **next steps**.
- This could include feedback to specific individuals or groups.

ACTION

The templates on the next two pages outline a simple format for recording focused evaluations.

Focused Evaluation

Subject	
Date	
Evaluators	
What is your focus?	
Key question/s?	

What evidence have you gathered?	What does it tell you?
Observation & teaching	
Work scrutiny	
Pupil discussion	
Assessment evidence	
Planning	
Other	

Focused Evaluation

Evaluation and outcomes What have we found?	
Action points What do we need to do next?	
Checking Has it made a difference? How do we know? Any follow up?	

Triangulating your evidence

Triangulating your evidence

When making judgements about the subject area that you lead, it is important that you gather information from a range of sources in order to reach a 'best fit' evaluation.

This is often called, 'triangulating your evidence'. In other words, taking evidence from a range of sources and checking that it presents a consistent picture. If it doesn't, you need to find out why not.

The diagram opposite identifies the types of evidence you may use, e.g.

- Teaching evidence: observations, drop ins, teacher feedback, evidence from planning, evidence from pupil work.
- Data evidence: assessment data
- Pupil evidence: conversations with pupils

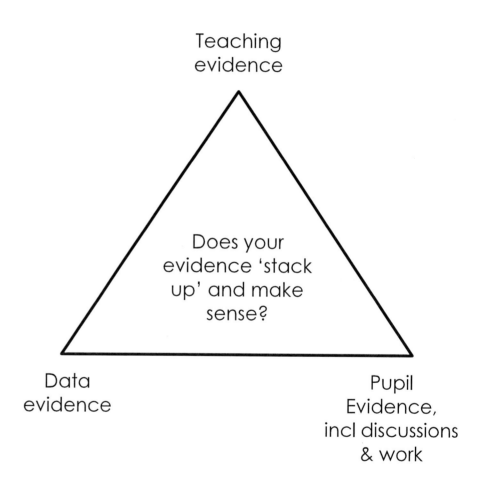

Teaching evidence

Does your evidence 'stack up' and make sense?

Data evidence

Pupil Evidence, incl discussions & work

Self-Evaluation Template

This section provides a simple template that school leaders can use to record the outcomes of their self evaluation.

Self evaluation

It is good practice for subject leaders to have a simple self-evaluation record in place. This helps subject leaders identify what is going well and what needs to be improved in the subject that they are responsible for leading.

This does not need to be an overly complicated document and should be short.

Many schools present these to governors.

The self-evaluation record and action plan should fit together.

The templates on the following pages may be useful as a starting point.

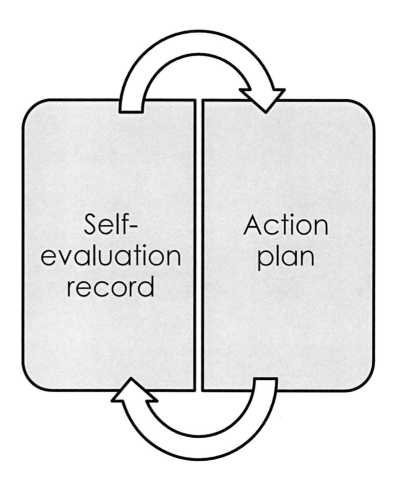

Self-Evaluation Statement

Subject	
Date	
Subject leader	

Strength and successes How do you know?	

	Evaluation	Evidence base	Next steps...
Achievement evaluation			
Teaching evaluation			
Curriculum evaluation			
Leadership evaluation			

Self-Evaluation Statement

Financial summary	
What resources are required?	

Subject leader summary

Subject	
Date	
Subject leader	

Past	Present	Future
What have we already achieved and improved?	Where are we now? What are the headlines from our self-evaluation?	Where are we heading? What are the key action points from the curriculum action plan?

Termly Subject Leader Update

Subject	Subject leader	Academic year	Term

	Areas of strength	Areas for development	Next steps
Planning			
Work sampling			
Lesson observation & drop ins			
Pupil interviews			
Curriculum coverage			
Assessment			
Other			

Action Planning

This section provides a simple template that school leaders can use to aid action planning.

Subject Leader Action Plan

Subject	Subject leader	Academic year

Objective (From self-evaluation)	Success criteria	Actions (who)	Time-scale	Resources/ training	Cost	Monitoring Note when actioned and how

Evaluation
(What has been the impact on outcomes and teaching?)

Questions for subject leaders

Questions for subject leaders

Many schools ask for a standard list of questions which subject leaders could consider, especially prior to an inspection. There is no standard list of questions to be used on inspection as it wholly depends on the school's own self evaluation, data and identified issues. If subject leaders consider the following model, they will be able to answer questions in all areas.

| How effective is … ? | How do you know? | What impact has your work had? | What are the next steps? |

The specific questions on the following pages may also help subject leaders to think through issues.

Standards, Progress & Achievement

- What proportion of pupils meet age related expectations?
- How has this changed as the cohort has moved through the school?
- How well do pupils achieve in this subject?
- Is there any difference based on analysis of groups? (e.g. SEN, more able, pupil premium etc.)
- How well do disadvantaged pupils and/or vulnerable pupils achieve?
- How do you evaluate standards?
- Based on your evaluation, what are your improvement points?
- What have you done which has had a positive impact on outcomes? How do you know?
- Which aspect of the subject do the pupils achieve best in?

Assessment

- How effective are your assessment arrangements? How accurate are assessments?
- How do you moderate assessments?
- How is assessment used? What impact does this have?
- How do you track progress? Is this consistent?
- What does your tracking tell you?

Teaching & Learning

❑ How effective is teaching & learning in the subject?

❑ Which are the strongest/weakest elements?

❑ What most needs improving? What are you doing to address this?

Curriculum

❑ Which aspects of the subject are the strongest?

❑ Which aspects most need improving? What are you doing to address this?

❑ How do you ensure that basic skills are applied across the curriculum?

❑ How does your subject impact on learning in other subjects?

❑ How is enrichment used to impact on learning?

❑ How does this subject promote fundamental British values?

❑ How does this subject promote and support spiritual, moral, social and cultural development?

Leadership

❑ How effective is your leadership? How can you evidence this?

❑ What has been the impact of your leadership?

❑ How do you communicate new issues & expectations to colleagues?

❑ What has improved most in the past year? Two years?

Monitoring and Evaluation

❑ How do you monitor and evaluate?

❑ What has your evaluation led to? What has been the impact?

❑ How do you make sure you are getting a true picture of what is happening?